THE SANGAI
The Pride of Manipur

THE SANGAI
The Pride of Manipur

L.M. Khaute

KALPAZ

The Sangai : The Pride of Manipur

Rs. 540

ISBN: 978-81-7835-772-0

Published in 2010 in India by
Kalpaz Publications
C-30, Satyawati Nagar,
Delhi-110052
e-mail: kalpaz@hotmail.com
Phone : 9212729499

Lasertype Setting by: Quick Media, Delhi
Printed at : Young Art Press, Delhi

Dedicated to the memories of my parents
Khaute Suangkhopau Vaiphei and Kholkhochin
whose lives... a saga of love, prayers and sacrifices for their children.

CONTENTS

ACKNOWLEDGEMENTS

I thank Mr Seiboi Singsit, IFS, Principal Chief Conservator of Forest; Mr Lamsei Baite, IFS; Mr L. Munindro Singh, IFS; Mrs Roui Kullai, IFS; Mr R.K. Nimai, IAS; Dr Kh. Shamungou; Mr S.C. Loitongba and Loktak Development Authority for their cooperation and support in finalizing my 'Sangai text'; Mr M. Shantikumar Singh, IPS; Mr I.K. Muivah, IPS; Mr Jason Shimray, MCS and Inspector K. Ngaraipam for their support in finalizing my 'Haofa text'; Mr Adon Vaiphei for his invaluable contribution; my Staff N. Jugol Singh; N. Saratchandra Singh; L. Indramani Sharma and Sambhu Pradhan for their valuable assistance; Pumkhosiam Khaute for Sangai sketch and finally, Mimi Khaute and my children for their backing. . .

L.M. Khaute

DEER SANGAI

A thousand years ago!
When the world was kinder and nobler
Than it ever was!
When love and romance echoed through the ages,
And when it was closer to the truth than ever before
With man and nature mingled in unison,
Thou were born, Oh! Deer Sangai.

The mind that hath conceived thee into what thou art,
Of grace, meekness, innocence and splendour,
Of the gentle noble soul of the wild world,
And a loving tender pride;
The hands that curved thy majestic antlers
And shaped thee into eternal beauty!
May praises be His! For His ingenuity!

Bliss was it in that wild of Siam and Shan,
Frolic was it in that wild,
Trolling thine way
From the Chindwin to the Loktak,
To find a new Haven like Heaven!
And like a flower afloat on the Loktak!
Captivating all that liveth! Oh! Deer Sangai.

L.M. Khaute

ODE TO THE LOKTAK LAKE

Oh, Loktak!
The legendary Water
With all thine grandeur;
The abode of the gods!
Where the gods charm the goddesses,
And play their flutes in tune with nature,
To the rhythm of dancing maidens,
And to enliven the souls that dwelleth!

A paradise to nature lovers!
An inspiration to the countless visitors;
The Life-giver to all that liveth;
A home to the Sangai;
The Enchantress to the creatures
That roameth the hills;
Into the kingdom of the Spirit of Nature,
Down the ages!

The Water of a proud civilization
That sustains all good things on this Land;
The gentle face of Manipur
That beams with love and kindness;
The hopes and dreams
That thou radiate down generations;
May thou endure until eternity!
Oh, immortal Lake!

LM Khaute

SECTION–A

PHOTO GALLERY

A Majestic Sangai

At the Second Home

Three Makes a Herd

A Curious Herd

Sangai Down the Years

Splendour of the Wild

A Classic Photo of a Sangai Herd

Sangai Head

Elegant Doe

An Adolescent Solitude

In Harmony with Nature

An Alert Herd

The Protective Male Sangai

Velvety Young Antlers...

Scurrying for Cover in
Keibul Lamjao National Park

Sangai Food Plants

Keibul Lamjao National Park

Sky, Land and Water at their Pristine Best

Fishing in a Misty Evening

A Crystalline Reflection of Sunset

Floating Abodes on the Lake

Sunset at the Loktak Lake

A Flock of Migratory Birds

Fishing in Serene Waters

Leisure at the Lake

Map of Manipur Showing Wildlife Protected Areas

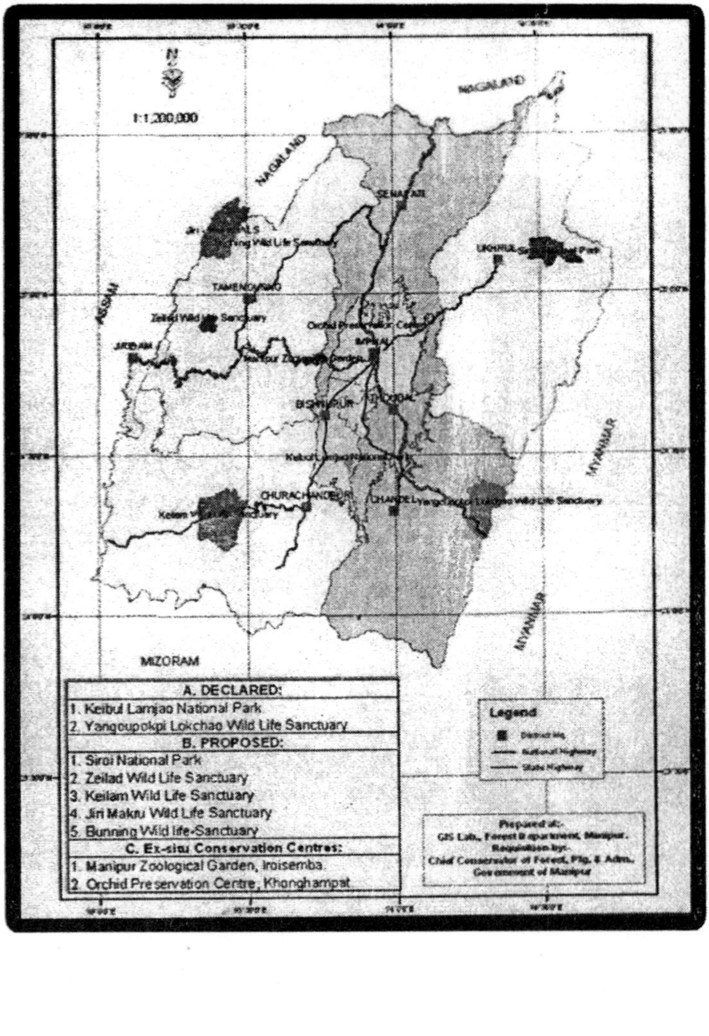

1

THE SANGAI AN INTRODUCTION

Manipur, the Land of the Sangai! Until the seventies, as far as I remember, most houses in the Kuki-Chin villages were adorned with heads of wild animals killed by hunters. It was part of the custom signifying accomplishment, skill, valour and pride. Those days, heads of animals were taken to the clan chief in a traditional way, with the accompaniment of a song called 'haanla' and 'gunfire'. This used to be an eventful occasion in a tribal life. 1960s.. As a boy, I was particularly impressed by the antlers of a deer, locally known as 'Sapeng', hung on the wall inside the house of Grandma Hoiting Vaiphei, Chief of Mualkot in Churachandpur District, about three kilometres south of Churachandpur town. My grandma, who died a centenarian, was a wise, dynamic, and kindhearted lady. She administered the village single-handedly for over five decades, as my grandpa had died early. She once said that in the early forties, wild animals, including the Sangai roamed around the marshy fields near the village. Those days, the forests were dense, and the plain areas swampy as the land could not be exploited due to scarce population. At one point, I had wondered whether the Sangai's domain ever extended to other parts of the State as this animal is known to have been confined only to its present sanctuary, Keibul Lamjao in the Loktak Lake.

In course of a tête-à-tête with Lamsei Baite IFS, Conservator of Forest, Manipur and some elderly persons, an interesting aspect of the Sangai habitation emerged. It was believed that this deer once roamed the Khuga valley. This is evident from a large number of heads of the animal preserved by hunters in Churachandpur District even today. A village has been christened 'Sangaikot', literally meaning the 'Sangai Corridor'. This village nestled between two mountain ranges along the Khuga round-road. Through this corridor, the Sangai crossed over from the Sugnu and Kumbi valley to Churachandpur (Khuga) valley and vice versa. Further, according to chiefs of Hengken and Khodang villages, the Sangai was found in the village forest of Hengken, Dongjang and Tuining areas during the early part of 1920. Those days, the villagers used to hunt Sangai and Hog deer from the village forest. Even today, the villagers preserve heads of a few Sangai by displaying them on the walls of their houses. The villagers said that the southern part of Keibul Lamjao was contiguously forested with wetland species like Phragmatis karka right upto Makhao area along the Imphal River. The Sangai would have reached these areas after crossing Sangaikot Hills, where human settlement was little. Since the fifties, there was no report of the Sangai migration in these areas. This could be due to the rapid increase in human population and conversion of wetland into paddy fields.

The Sangai today is an endangered species. While in Bishnupur District as Superintendent of

Police in 1993, I often toured the Loktak Lake and Keibul Lamjao areas to watch the Sangai. I was told that to sight the deer, sometimes, one has to trek the sanctuary for hours. The rare moments I spent with the Sangai were while visiting the Iroishemba Zoological Garden and the Second Home in January 2008 with family and friends. The pages that follow hereafter bespeak an animal lover's sincere quest to discover the multi-faceted characteristics of this indigenous yet elegant deer of Manipur, dearly known by the name 'Sangai.'

2

THE SANGAI, THE BROW-ANTLERED DEER OF MANIPUR (Cervus eldi eldi-M'Clelland)

The Sangai is a noble wildlife! The name 'Sangai' was coined from the unique posture adopted by the deer while running. The deer particularly the male would stop momentarily after running some distance and then would begin to run again as if he is waiting for his mate or someone else. The name Sangai is derived from the word 'Sa' meaning 'animal' and 'ngai' meaning 'waiting-while-looking-on'. The Manipur Sangai is a rare and unique mammal and is one of the most beautiful deer on this planet. It is also known to the people of Manipur as the 'Dancing Deer'. The deer is a popular subject in local folklore and dance tradition. Wildlife lovers across the continent have written a number of books on unique animal species. It is widely accepted that except in the Southeast Asia, which is known to be home to three distinctive species of Elds Deer, the brow-antlered deer is not found elsewhere. The Sangai belongs to one of the three subspecies of Elds Deer. The other two subspecies are Myanmar's brow-antlered deer or Thamin (Cervus eldi thamin). The Thamin (Cervus eldi thamin) is found in upper and lower Myanmar as well as in western Thailand, and the Siamese brow-antlered deer (Cervus eldi siamensis) in eastern Thailand and on the island of Hainan. It is widely believed that these three subspecies of deer were once the same species. The Cervus eldi siamensis was at first believed to have existed in Thailand and later migrated to Myanmar. Here it assumed the name Cervus eldi thamin after it had undergone certain physical changes. Later, the Cervus eldi thamin moved further to Manipur and acquired a few more distinctive characteristics before it assumed its present name Cervus eldi eldi (Brow-antlered Deer).

3

MORPHOLOGICAL STUDY

The Sangai is considered a medium-sized deer and measures about 100-110 cm in length. The stag measures about 115-125 cm in height at the shoulder and weighs about 95-110 kilograms. A doe is shorter and lighter than a stag. The length of the deer from its tail to its ear is about 145-155 cm. The Sangai has a short tail and does not have a prominent rump.

The beauty of the Sangai lies in its antlers, capturing the imagination of poets, animal lovers and story-tellers down the years. The Sangai has a distinctive crown of antlers measuring 100-110 cm in length with a very long brow line, which forms the main beam so that the two form a continuous curve at right angles. True to its name, i.e., brow-antlered deer, the forward protruding beams appear to be coming out from the eyebrows. The antlers are asymmetrical. Initially, the beams are straight; however, with gradual increase in the length and the beams getting forked, they also get more and more curved. As the beams grow, tines (branches of a stag's antlers) gradually emerge and form an inward curve. The horns branch out majestically into antlers to form a crown on the deer's head like an exquisite piece of craftsmanship. The stag sheds its antlers every year between late June and early September. This annual phenomenon takes place to mark the completion of the estrous cycle (periodic state of sexual excitement in females) wherein the antlers played an instrumental role in attracting and luring females into mating as well as defending its sexual dominance. Once the mating season is over, the stag no longer needs its antlers until the next mating season.

The Sangai has coarse hair, the colour of which changes according to season. In winter, the deer's matted coat particularly that of a full-grown stag changes from brown to dark brown. Similarly, the doe's coat changes from light brown to dark brown, albeit with a comparatively lighter hue. In both the male and female, the hair is smooth and thin yet uneven in length. The underparts are normally pale brown in colour. The young have brown spotted-hair, traces of which can also be seen in adults up to two to three years. The Sangai has splayed hoofs. Its sister subspecies Thamins and Siamensis, however, do not have splayed hoofs. Its legs are slender; its hoofs can be spread out. This special adaptation facilitates movement in its swampy habitat of floating phumdi in the Keibul Lamjao Sanctuary (now National Park). This is the secret behind the Sangai's survival in the swamp.

4

REPRODUCTIVE BEHAVIOUR

The life span of the Sangai is about sixteen years. It attains its sexual maturity when it is four years old. The female Sangai can reproduce until it attains the age of ten years. The rutting period is from late January or early February to May, and the normal gestation period is 245-273 days. The deer breeds once in a year. Breeding lasts from the month of September to December. A doe delivers only one fawn at a time unlike other animals. It takes two to three weeks for the fawn to begin walking on its own.

Studies have shown that during the gestation period, the females average ten to seventeen estrous cycles, and after mating females enter the anestrous cycle, during which they are not sexually active. It is also observed that ovarian functions in females are activated by the presence of males. The deer is a seasonal breeder and its peak breeding season is March. The males are generally very aggressive before they enter into mating, but not so during the peak period of the rutting season. There is no sign of the adult female showing preference to adult male. The Sangai prefers to move about from one place to another during the rutting period. When a stag raises its head upwards and displays the incisors, it is considered an act of aggressiveness. In Keibul Lamjao, it is observed that the Sangai rubs its head or pre-orbital organ on the bushes and hits the bushes violently with its forelegs or antlers. Rutting fights are enacted to determine the rank of the stag – who will dominate who. A solitary stag shows the tendency to be a little more hostile than the others towards another grown-up stag. This would either invite a confrontation from its rival or ensure its rival's exit from the scene out of fear. These fights normally take place during the months of February and March. During the fights, the deer interlock their antlers and fight very violently. To regain strength in the middle of the fights, the stags would move a little backward to resume the fights moments later. The victor stag raises its head with a great sense of pride and the vanquished lowers its head and then leaves the scene. This habit of fighting has led to a number of deaths. As per official records, two stags lodged in the Manipur Zoological Garden died in March 1990 after fighting over possession of a receptive doe.

A stag pursues a doe by showing intimidating posture till she experiences the peak of its heat. This behaviour is generally observed for about 48-hour duration. During this duration, the doe would respond to the stag's gestures. When the female is ready to reciprocate to the overtures of the male, she would rub her nose against the flanks of the male while keeping its hind legs apart and lowering its head. Then the stag climbs on her, thrusting its forelegs straight on her body and resting its head on the doe's withers with its tail straightened downwards. The male would then gradually raise its body till its legs are straight up. The mating lasts a few moments. After the mating is over, the male is content and calm, whereas the female flaps its ears in quick succession and wiggles its tail.

5

'THE DANCING DEER'

The Sangai is the essence of life in Manipur and the pride of the Land. It has charmed and endeared itself to the people since many years. Many had sung its praises, composed poems, written about its uniqueness, and it is a subject of folk tales down the years. It exists only in this tiny fringe of India bordering Myanmar. The movement of this deer in the floating biomass (phumdi) is very peculiar. Instead of bounding with fore and hind feet coming on the ground at the same time, it seems to be proceeding on its hind legs, the body being held almost vertical. This action prevents it from sinking in the quagmire and enables it to move about with ease on the floating phumdi. This graceful posture and unique movement have impelled some deer lovers to call it the 'Dancing Deer of Manipur'. No other animal is known to possess this artistic yet clever maneuverability and survive in such unique habitat for generations.

6

POPULATION

The population of Sangai is very fragile. As per available data, in the year 1955, Sangai population was estimated to be one hundred animals. In 1975, during the first aerial census a small herd of fourteen deer (6 stags, 5 hinds, and 3 fawns) were found living in the Keibul Lamjao Park. However, with the declaration of Keibul Lamjao as a national park and subsequent protection and conservation measures taken up by the State Government, the deer population has increased substartially. In 1977, another aerial survey was carried out, which revealed the presence of eighteen animals. During the last aerial census carried out in 1993, ninety eight animals were counted.

Later, the census method was switched over to 'ground census', and since the year 1994, ground census has been held almost every year. Ground census is difficult during rainy season. The best time for carrying out ground census is from February to April when the vegetation gets dried and the phumdi settles on the lake bed. The Forest Department adopted a simple method of conducting ground survey–counting simultaneously from vantage posts, viz. Toya Hill, Pabot Hills, Chingmai, Sagram, Keibul Hills, etc. At each vantage point the deer is counted with the help of powerful binoculars between 4 p.m. and 5 p.m. followed by the next day between 6 a.m. and 7 a.m. The ground survey carried out in 1994 revealed the presence of about one hundred and thirty-seven animals in the sanctuary. It was noticed that there seemed to be considerable variation in the population figure arrived at through aerial and ground survey. However, the Forest Department is affirmative that the Sangai population is steadily increasing. In March 1995, one hundred and fifty-two Sangai (58 stags (male), 69 hinds (female) and 25 fawns) were found to inhabit the park along with one hundred and eighteen hog deer and one hundred wild boars. In 2000, its number increased to one hundred and sixty-two. During the latest survey in 2003, the deer's population was estimated to be one hundred and eighty animals (65 stags, 74 hinds and 41 fawns). It is estimated that the animal's population grows by 9 per cent per annum. During the period 1977 to 2003, the sex ratio was between fifty-five males per one hundred females and one hundred and three males per one hundred females, respectively. In 1999, the number of males was higher than that of the females. The mean sex ratio, however, stands 79.4 (2.5) males per 100 does. The doe to fawn ratio was 37.1 (3.8) fawn per 100 does.

These figures show how endangered this species is today. The deer is extremely vulnerable to natural calamities like floods, earthquake, wildfire and animal epidemic. The *Sangai* was reported extinct in 1951, but after being rediscovered in July 1954, it has finally become Keibul Lamjao's prime attraction.

7

FAVOURITE FOOD PLANTS

In Keibul Lamjao National Park, the Sangai feeds on a diet consisting mainly of food plants such as *Learsia hexandra (Hup), Carex cruciata (Hundung), Echinochloa stegnia (Hupkha), Capillipedium spp. (Wanamanbi), Zizania latifolia (Ishing-kambong), Cynodon dactylon (Tingthou), Panicus humidorum (Kangmapal), Brachiaria mutica (Paragrass)*, etc. These grass species grow in abundance throughout the park. Sprouts of these grasses start growing during late winter and after a spell of monsoon rain, they grow fully. During this period, the deer needs wholesome food for growth of its antlers and its foetus. The Sangai begins foraging for food from early daybreak till about

8 a.m. The deer rests under bushy reeds and grasses when the heat rises at day time. It resumes feeding from late afternoon (3 p.m. - 4 p.m.) till mid evening (5 p.m. - 6 p.m.). Normally, on bright sunny days, it feeds only till about 7 a.m. whereas on cloudy days, it feeds till about 10 a.m. At night, even the hillocks are used as resting places. The herd of Sangai in Keibul Lamjao have cleverly adapted themselves to their environment and synchronized their reproductive cycle with availability of food.

8

KEIBUL LAMJAO, THE ONLY NATURAL HABITAT OF THE SANGAI

Keibul Lamjao has its origin in history. Once upon a time, the King of Moirang secretly held a Meitei King (referred to as 'Kei', meaning 'tiger') captive, with hands tied at this place. Since then the place came to be known as 'Keipunba' or 'Keibul'. This place was the favourite habitat of tigers or kei in the past, especially during dry season and hence, acquired the name 'Keibul' or 'Keipunpham' in due course of time.

The park is situated at 32.56 km (as the crow flies) south of the Manipur State capital, Imphal in India.The park spreads over to an area of about forty kilometres and is situated in the south-eastern side of the Loktak Lake. The Loktak Lake is situated at a distance of 25.01 km (crow-fly) from Imphal and has an area of 70.11 sq.km (appro). Experts have broadly divided the park into three distinct types: - (i) areas covered under phumdi at the central, western and southern direction (ii) the three hillocks, viz. Toyaching, Pabotching and Chingjao and the grasslands at the ridges of the Thangbirel and Bora-yangbi, and (iii) the northern deepwater with or without phumdi (aquatic ecosystem). The park lies at 24° 27′ - 24° 31′ N latitude, 93° 53′ E - 93° 55′E longitude, and at an altitude of 767m-788m. Its temperature is 4°C (January) - 32°C (June), and humidity - 45 per cent (March) - 80 per cent (August). The temperatures here range from 1.7°C to 34.4°C, and the annual rainfall recorded is 1220 mm. Maximum humidity of about 81 per cent is experienced in August, and in March there is about 49 per cent humidity. Now Keibul Lamjao is renowned for being the only protected floating wildlife sanctuary in the world. The Sangai are confined in a small area of about nine to ten square kilometres in the southern side of the park. They are hardly seen in the north-eastern side of the park because of the clear water, absence of phumdi and proximity to human habitation. In 1966, Keibul Lamjao was converted into a sanctuary and officially declared a national park on March 28, 1977. Although the park is about 25.81 square kilometres approximately surrounded by marshes, hillocks and water, the core area covered by phumdi is only about 9.5 square kilometres, where Sangai can dwell. A number of streams converged at the park, and this combined with the vast marshes turned the park into a spectacular wetland. The Keibul Lamjao Park, which is part of the Loktak Lake, is covered almost totally by floating mats of dense aquatic grass, known locally as 'phumdi'. Eighty per cent of the biomass is submerged, and the vegetation forms a 90-120 cm thick grass on the water surface. About half a century ago, the predominant plants that constituted 'phumdi' were Tou (45 per cent), Singut (25 per cent) and Khoimom (15 per cent). The composition of vegetation here has undergone rapid changes, and it is now estimated that large numbers of Hoop leersia hexandra and Sing kambong Zizania latifolia, a protein-rich plant often used as food, sprung up all over. The park is incredibly rich in flora, which includes wild grasses and a kind of wild rice. The type of forest in the sanctuary is moist semi-evergreen forest and a combination of aquatic, wetland and terrestrial ecosystem. The most common aquatic plants that grow and make the park unique and the ideal habitat of the Sangai include *Cynodon dactylon (Tingthou), Alpinia galanga (Pullei), Eichornia crassipes (Kabokang), Hedychium coronarium (Loklei), Zizania latifolia (Ishing kambong), Saccharum munja (Khoimom), S. bengalensis, Eiranthus procerus (Singnang), Dioschoria bulbifera (Phumha), Nelumbo nucifera (Thambal), Phragmites karka (Tou),* and many more plants.

A fascinating way to see the park is by boating in the early morning or in the evening when the lake is most enchanting. The deer live in small herds and lie low most of the day, only to come out to feed either at dawn or at dusk. This behaviour is intriguing for wildlife watchers. Local boatmen act as guides for tourists, and take them around the sanctuary and the lake. For most people, the best time to enjoy the park is between 6 a.m. and 10 a.m. and 3.30 p.m. and 6 p.m. There are observation towers in the park. From these towers, one can have a good view of the *S*angai and the park. Besides, a visitor can opt for a more exciting and adventurous guided tour through the park. Visitors must take care while stepping on the floating biomass to prevent mishaps as the water beneath is deep and cold. They are also advised to watch out for snakes and reptiles.

In 1908, Hudson had likened the valley of Manipur to a paradise for sports lovers. In his words, "In the cold weather, the numerous lakes and jheels are covered with wild duck, teal, geese, snipe, and in the hills woodcocks and rare pheasants are to be found. The eastern edges of the Loktak Lake afford a home to the brow-antlered deer, while the fastnesses and thickets of the lofty mountain peaks shelter the serao".

Besides the Sangai, other animals in the park include Otter, Civet, Wild boar, Sambar, Muntjac and Hog deer.

A primitive primate, the slow Loris is found in scattered pockets in the hills. The Assamese stump-tailed macaques and the Hoolock gibbon are also found in the western hills. The Rhesus monkey also inhabits the area. The large Indian civet (Viverra zibetha) and small Indian civet (Viverricula indica), common Otter (Lutra lutra) and Wild boar (Sus scrofa) are some of the large mammals that inhabit the State forest. A rare wildcat species like the Marbled cat and Temminck's golden cat are often sighted in the mountains surrounding the lake. The Himalayan black bear and the Malayan bear are also seen occasionally in the mountain wilderness foraging for food.

A wide range of rare birds dwell in the Loktak. In winter, waterfowl and other birds migrate to the lake from different places. Nowadays, due to human interference and limited open water space for the birds to splash around, the Loktak, it is said, is no longer the idyllic habitation it used to be in the earlier times. The White stork, Black eagle, Hooded crane, Falcon, Bamboo partridge, a number of small reed-dwelling birds and green Peafowl live in the lake and make the park spectacular and buzzing. Some of the species of Hornbills found here include the Brownbacked hornbill, Rufous-necked hornbill, etc. Some of the common invertebrates are common lizard, cobra, krait, viper, python, tortoise, fishes, etc.

9

THE SANGAI DOWN THE YEARS

The natural history of wildlife in Manipur is built upon a few sporadic records in the 19th century and is still to take a concrete shape. In 1838, Percy Eld gave a scientific account of the Sangai in his sporting diary as a nondescript species of deer. His article on the Sangai appeared in the Calcutta Journal of Natural History in 1841, and the deer was named Cervus eldi eldi by M'Clelland in 1842. Percy Eld in his sporting diary of 21st May 1841 says, "The sungraee, (Imphal East Sangai) it is called by the natives or larger deer of Munipore (Manipur) is only to be found in the valley of that state, but neither in Cachar, nor the Kabo valley, nor in any of the Naga Hills surrounding Munipore. Its favourite haunts are low grass and swamps round the edge of the Loktak Lake at the western end of the valley, and the marshy ground at the foot of the hills". This provides useful information about the animal when not much about it was written or heard of.

History bears witness to the importance attached to wildlife conservation by the British rulers as well as by the Kings. In the pre-1709 period, there were no laws to control hunting and killing of animals. Hence, even in Keibul Lamjao any body could hunt any animal, including Sangai. As is evident from our folklore and other historical evidences, the Keibul Lamjao area has been home to the Sangai from time immemorial. In 1841, Lt Percy Eld, Assistant to the Commissioner of Assam wrote, "It is gregarious in its habits, and after the annual grass-burning, I have frequently seen herds of two or three hundred." (Eld, 1841, cited in Gee, 1960). Alhon Wilson (1924) had recorded that prior to 1841 the Sangai was "preserved by order of the royal family, and any man, who was proved to have killed one had his hand chopped off. But after they took over the affairs of the State, the deer were allowed to take their chance. Luckily, a sporting Political Agent finally issued orders to preserve this rare species from indiscriminate slaughter..." (Cited in Gee, 1960). In the year 1934, the Manipur State Durbar passed a resolution prohibiting shooting of Sangai to prevent its extinction. For protection of game animals and birds, the rulers believed that the predator must go. Tigers and leopards were classified as vermin and suitable rewards were given to those responsible for their killing. There are records which testify that whenever the King came to know about a tiger on the prowl endangering human lives, the king himself rushed to the affected place to deal with the situation. The King would reward handsomely any person who informed him about such incident. According to Higgins a reward of Rs. 2,077 was paid to the hill men during 1915-1916 for destruction of 19 tigers, 72 leopards and 315 bears. Royal Chronicles contained records of 322 tigers killed during Maharaja Chandrakirti during 1850-1886. These records talked about capture of elephants from several forests of the State, especially from the Koubru, Jiri and Leimatak forest. In a single trip, the Maharaja was said to have captured more than 60 elephants.

In the fifties, the Sangai was considered extinct in Manipur. The fate of the Sangai was very uncertain those days notwithstanding enforcement of Game Rules and regulation of hunting. In 1950, EP Gee, the then Hony. Secretary, Eastern Zone of Indian Board for Wild Life declared Sangai extinct and that there was no necessity to establish a wildlife sanctuary then. However, EP Gee rediscovered a remnant herd of six deer in Keibul Lamjao area in one early morning of October 1959 that led to the creation of the national park later. Dwelling on the uniqueness of the ecosystem of Keibul Lamjao as the deer's habitat in 1961, he quoted Lt. Col. HS Wood, "No other animal could exist in such swamps...The action of this deer is very peculiar. Instead of bounding with fore and hind feet coming on the ground at the same time, it seems to be proceeding on its hind legs, the body being held almost vertical. This action prevents it from sinking in the quagmire." The English gentlemen who keenly studied the Sangai's traits and wrote about this animal would always be remembered particularly by the people of Manipur for their invaluable contribution towards a better understanding and appreciation of the Sangai.

The Sangai occupies a number of pages in the history of Manipur. Kings and nobles too were enamoured with this animal. There were strict royal orders for the preservation of this animal, and drastic actions, including chopping off the hands of a person who killed the deer, were imposed before 1891 (Wilson, 1891). The Games Rules of Manipur State 1931 (Draft Rules 1974) was enacted to safeguard the deer. With the enactment of the Wildlife (Protection) Act 1972 (Manipur Rules 1974) Sangai conservation has received a fresh impetus. In the same year, the Manipur Government declared Keibul Lamjao area as Reserved Forests under the Indian Forest Act 1927. In 1975, during an aerial survey carried out by the State Forest Department, fourteen heads were counted. On 5th April 1977, Keibul Lamjao was declared as 'National Park.'

Today, due to conservation efforts made by the State Forest Department, the number of the Sangai has risen from a meagre fourteen in 1975 to over one hundred and eighty.

10

SANGAI FOLKLORE

"The Sangai figured prominently in the Manipuri folklore and is a glittering gem in the rich heritage of Manipur," says Dr Kh. Shamungou, a noted Sangai researcher. It is said that a legendary hero, Kadeng Thangjahanba of Moirang once captured and brought a lovely Sangai from Torbung Lamjao to be a memorable gift for his beloved Tonu Laijinglembi. However, when all hopes of their conjugal sojourn were shattered by misfortune, the hero in a pang of separation parted the deer in the wild of Keibul Lamjao. Since then, the place has been the only home of the Sangai.

11

ROYAL BOAT AND SANGAI HEAD

In the Manipuri folklore, Pudangkoi Khukoiba of the Luwang clan had, by the grace of a divine entity, transformed himself into a deer that was to be called 'Sangai'. The ancient literature like Hijin Hirao and Hirol talked about the making of 'Hiyang Hiren' (Royal Boat) by the Luwang King Punshiba. One day while strolling, the king saw a strange and unusual sight of locusts, ants and rats crossing the river in flood with the help of dry twigs and logs. This aroused the King's enthusiasm, and he then designed a boat. Thus was born the first 'Hiyang Hiren'. On the auspicious day of inauguration of the boat, the King placed the head of the Sangai on the front of the boat as a mark of dedication to his dearest brother. According to another story, the Sangai deer transformed by Pudangkoi was killed by his son, placed on the head of the boat and brought home. From that day onwards, it was customary to decorate every Royal Boat with the Sangai head bearing a crown of long antlers.

12

CHALLENGES TO SANGAI CONSERVATION

Conservation of the Sangai is of paramount importance. It is widely felt that the government and its citizens have great responsibilities towards the wellbeing of animals. According to Mahatma Gandhi, "The greatness of a nation and its moral progress can be judged by the way its animals are treated."

Conservation of the Sangai is closely linked with preservation of phumdis, the floating masses in the Keibul Lamjao National Park. Nearly one third of thc park is covered by phumdi. It has been observed that the grassland and phumdis have undergone some kind of degradation over the years. Productivity of the phumdi is believed to be influenced by the depth of the water. Tall and green fodder gradually dwindled because of the intense competition for grazing on the dried phumdi. This has affected the load-taking capacity of the Keibul Lamjao Sanctuary. The Loktak Project and Ithai Barrage have often been attributed to causing dislocation to the ideal rutting environment in the park. An increase in the water volume of the Loktak Lake has resulted in a decrease in the thickness of phumdi. Studies have shown that during floods, the animal died in large numbers due to sudden alteration in the structure and composition of phumdi. A study carried out by a team of Forest Officials led by Mr. S. Singsit, IFS, Principal Chief Conservator of Forest, Manipur that included, among others, Dr. S.A. Hussain of the Wildlife Institute of India, Dehradun concluded that that there has been a significant change in the composition of the phumdi, which is prominent with respect to *Phragmites karka, Zizania latifolia and Saccharum munja* (favourite food of Sangai). The study further stated that in 1960, EP Gee recorded a maximum density of *Phragmites* karka (45 per cent) followed by *Narenga porphyrochroma* (25 per cent), *Saccharum munja* (15 per cent) and other species namely *Zizania latifolia, Alpinia allughas and Erianthus procerus* in the range of two to five percent in the phumdi. During 1980s, the ratio between shelter and food plants was about sixty percent and forty percent. The present conditions favour growth of food plants like *Learsia hexandra and Capillipedium spp.* The shelter plants are stunted mainly due to constant floating of phumdi, making the Sangai vulnerable to poaching.

It has also been observed that deforestation, jhumming and faulty land management at the catchment area of the Loktak Lake and its surrounding hills result in soil erosion and increased silt. There had often been wildfire in the park during dry season leading to deterioration in the deer's natural habitat. These developments will also adversely influence the climate and environment and might some day cause the lake to dry up. Imagine, the Sangai without marshes! The Forest Department is monitoring vegetation of the park; the unwanted weeds are eradicated and species suitable for food and shelter for Sangai are planted. Controlled burning at strategic points is carried out. Raised earthen platforms are provided for the deer to take shelter in case of flash flood. Rock salts are provided at selected places for mineral supplement to the animals. Further, at Chingmei, watch towers and facilities for visitors are constructed. Besides, certain plant species and trees are planted for the Sangai.

The local people have often used pesticides and insecticides such as DDT, BHC, etc., for fishing and catching wild birds in the sanctuary. The Loktak is one of the primary sources of living for the local people, who carry out fishing, collect firewood, fodder, grass, vegetables, etc., from here on a day-to-day basis. The Lake has become a common habitat for man and animal, and the nature of such coexistence is determined by man and not by the Sangai. These activities, therefore, not only affect the deer's reproductive behaviour, but also endanger living things in the park, including the deer. For effective control and protection of the Sangai from poachers and also to check infiltrators, cutting and maintenance of channels are taken up regularly for making easy mobility of the patrolling staff. Fire lines are maintained in the park to check fire hazards during census operation. To prevent infiltrators from entering inside the National Park, to win trust and confidence of the villagers and to generate income, the Wildlife Wing is distributing bee boxes, fish fingerlings, seedlings, sewing machines and chullahs, and drilling hand pumps, etc.

A major fire never witnessed before broke out in Keibul Lamjao National Park in the early hours of February 22, 2009, which eventually spread to Nongmaiching, Ngakhapat, Haorang side and Toya Hill. Almost three quarters of the park have been ravaged by the fire. There was no Sangai casualty; however, at about 5.30 pm Sangai herd were seen running beyond the fire lines made by the Forest Department from the Watch towers.

Due to its small population and limited area of habitation, the Sangai procreates through an inbreeding process. This system of breeding is likely to give rise to genetic disorders among the fawns and may even lead to its eventual extinction. A scientific study of the animal will help in conservation of the species in the long run Poaching is another threat to the deer. Watch towers have been constructed for detection of fire and infiltrators and poachers. Although killing of the Sangai is prohibited, the deer continue to be under threats from poachers as the heads have a high decorative value. The beautiful antlers have thus increased the threats against the deer from hunters. One common method adopted by hunters is to lay traps. On a number of occasions, such illegal activities were detected and a few deer have been rescued. In 1998 two trapped deer were reportedly rescued in the park, but they did not survive. "Humans are the only hunters who kill when not hungry", says Steven Spielberg. In this case too, hunger obviously was not the force that had driven man to kill the animal. Pythagoras, the mathematician also says, "For as long as men massacre animals, they will kill each other! Indeed, he who sows the seed of murder and pain cannot reap joy and love". Think about it!

Due to constant human and cattle intrusion into the park and its proximate areas, there are chances of communicable diseases breaking out in the sanctuary. If such a thing happens, it may be a difficult situation to deal with, and failure to contain the problem timely could lead to a catastrophe. To prevent communicable diseases like FMD from domestic cattle, immunization of the domestic cattle are carried out at different centres of the surrounding villages. Further, free medical camps are also regularly conducted at the surrounding villages of the park. On a number of occasions, the Law Enforcement Agencies had to launch major combing operations in the Keibul Lamjao National Park and its surroundings in the Loktak Lake under compelling circumstances, thereby often disrupting normal activities of the animal. An atmosphere conducive to natural existence of the deer in the park is required to be created by all concerned agencies, groups or individuals for the sake of the Sangai.Animals are endangered because of human encroachment.

They can survive the threat of extinction if we address the individual problems each ecosystem faces by providing people with the basic necessities of life: food, water, shelter, income and education. When people have options, animals have hope. Give someone in need an option to poaching and killing endangered wildlife. Hence, conservation should start with children.

Further, every ecosystem has a unique problem that affects the people, the animals and the environment, as below:

- Burning land causes habitat destruction
- Lack of education creates myths and encourages poaching
- The desire to own exotic pets promotes illegal pet trade
- Lack of clean water and sanitation spreads disease among people and animal.

For achieving long-term support for conservation of Keibul Lamjao National Park and the Sangai and encouraging real appreciation of the ecosystem, it is essential to gain widespread support from all segments of people. The park has high potential to support tourism and become an ideal centre for nature education and recreation. Therefore, the government has taken up a comprehensive set of activities as follows:

- Nature Interpretation Hall, where interpretation materials brochures, leaflets, etc. are available.
- Kitchen Hall for tourists
- Restrooms
- Tourist Huts/Hawa Mahal
- Tourist Market Centre
- Rest House

Awareness campaigns have been initiated. Wildlife week, seminar, workshop, conservation week, essay and drawing competitions are held regularly.

The Wildlife Institute of India takes up a study on the population dynamics of the Sangai along with its associate animals. Census throws light on distribution of animals, their population and changes in population in different zones. In fact, spatial analysis of census data with respect to suitability of habitat in terms of availability of food, shelter, etc., may also help in deciding set of management prescriptions.

Research adds to the existing knowledge and removes or reduces uncertainty. At present, researchers from the Wild Life Institute of India, Dehradun are conducting various research activities on DNA of the Sangai, vegetation analysis of habitat, population dynamics and socio-economic status under the active guidance of Dr S.A. Hussain and Mrs Ruchi Badola of the Wild Life Institute of India.

Construction of quarters, barracks, offices, compound wall, water reservoir, etc., are some of the activities taken up under infrastructure development.

13

RECENT STEPS TO SAVE THE SANGAI ELESWHERE

A number of initiatives have been taken up by different people towards the cause of the Sangai. The recent nationwide 'Save Sangai Campaign' launched on the 30th of July 2008 by Imphal-based NGOs 'For a better Manipur', 'Northeast India Biodiversity' and 'Northeast Centre for Environmental Education and Research' is one ambitious venture initiated by the public to save the deer from extinction. As per newspaper reports, the campaign was first held at India Gate in New Delhi, Gateway of India in Mumbai, Lalbagh in Bangalore and the Marina Beach in Chennai. About 100 volunteers participated and they distributed pamphlets with the aim to create awareness about the Sangai and the dangers faced by this species. It has also been reported that people living around the Keibul Lamjao National Park have set up an organization called the 'Environmental Social Reformation and the Sangai Protection Forum' (ESRSPF) with its branches all over the State.

The Sangai Forum volunteers are learnt to keep a close watch over signs of danger and activities detrimental to the Sangai. They organize search parties to locate deer in danger inside the parkand look out for poachers and organize awareness programmes in villages. The Forum volunteers also work with forest officials and forest guards to save the deer.

The Sangai has been included in the list of endangered species and its hunting has been prohibited under Schedule I of the Wildlife Protection Act 1972. The IUCN Red Data Book has described the deer as "Critically Endangered". It has also been listed in Appendix-1 of the Convention on International Trade in Endangered Species (CITES).

Significance attached to this animal is growing steadily. In 1989 at Nandankanan in Orissa, the

Sangai was named 'Species of the Year'. In the 100th year celebration of Mysore Zoo, experts from different places discussed the Sangai and its conservation under the banner 'Our Sangai'. In 1992, British Airways adopted a slogan, "Conservation of Your Sangai is now our Business Also".

The following suggestions may help in the Sangai conservation. An institute named after the Sangai may be set up to foster, fund, promote Sangai conservation research, education and wildlife resource protection. There are a number of bodies all over the world committed to the task of wildlife conservation and are untiringly working towards this goal. The Slate Foundation, the Owens Foundation for Wildlife Conservation, the Wildlife Conservation Network, the Common Sense Environmental Fund (CSEF), etc., are among the many-noted organizations often heard about. These bodies believe that conservation starts with children, seek to be the foremost bodies preventing cruelty to animals and advancing education and science so that solutions are evolved for the unique problems of every ecosystem that affect the people, the animals and the environment. Their mission also seeks to bring about a world where wildlife is abundant and extinction is rare and a world where people esteem wildlife and recognize the importance of biological diversity to their own well-being.

A strong dedicated Sangai Protection Force may be set up with the following tasks:

- To protect the deer from poachers, anti-social elements, and other forms of interference from man and animals.
- To coordinate with forest and police authorities, NGOs and individuals associated with protection of the deer.
- To assess the environment and developments likely to have a bearing on safety of the deer and take up suitable.
- To monitor outbreaks of epidemic among men and cattle living in the nearby areas of the sanctuary and subsequently take measures to prevent further spread of the epidemic among the deer population.

The State Government may adopt a vibrant policy for conservation of the Sangai that may include among other things scientific research on the Sangai, ecology, education, awareness campaign, protection, breeding, alternative sanctuaries for the deer, environmental fund and conservation network.

Being an indigenous deer, the Sangai should take the pride of place in Manipur. The State abounds with rich flora and fauna. An ideal *alternative habitat* for the Sangai may soon be identified so that it survives to remain the 'Pride of Manipur'.

The Sangai is a gift to mankind! The history of co-existence between man and wildlife is replete with tales of struggles for survival through the ages. In this twenty-first century wherein man rules the roost, it has become his sacred duty to protect wildlife for the sake of ecological harmony conceived for the Creation. The Sangai will enrich our planet and make it a lovelier place to live in!

Let us save the Sangai for posterity. Our children deserve it.

SECTION–B

A TALE OF THE THANGJING HILLS (A Short Story for Children)

Many years ago, in a village in the Thangjing foothills lived two families. They had strong ties. Boynao, a six-year old boy and his friend, Boipu a five-year old symbolized the friendship between the families. The village was inhabited by people of different communities. People of the village were united and forward-looking. Agriculture was the mainstay of the village economy. One third of the population practised jhum cultivation whereas two thirds took up fishing and cultivation. Boynao belonged to a fisherman's family and Boipu to a jhum cultivator's.

One fine winter day, Boynao and Boipu ventured into the Thangjing Hills out of sheer adventure. It was early in the morning! Their trip began with excitement! They never saw beyond the foothills. For them, the jungle was shrouded in myth and mystery. The little boys had heard stories of fairies, spirits, wild animals and reptiles, especially python living in the Thangjing Hills from their grandparents. The way up was dense forest, misty, rocky, dark and inhospitable. As they inched their way up, they heard unusual and frightening sounds of insects and wild animals. Moments later, they sighted the hornbills, eagles, parrots and jungle fowls. The birds greeted them with their songs. They were charmed! Boipu said that the jungle was more enchanting than their village. Boynao, however, felt that much more excitement was still to come.

After awhile, they came across a patch of water. It was like an oasis in the vast expanse of the Sahara desert. It was located on the slope of the hill they were climbing. The urge to discover the secrets of the jungle brought them this far. They were tired and thirsty. They drank the water trickling down the rocky slope. The water was as sparkling as diamond. It was like a spectacular miniature lake. Soon they discovered that it was the main attraction of birds and animals. The lake was replenished continuously by cascades on the steep mountain with the sound of music to the tune of nature. After sometime, they heard the sound of birds hovering over the water. The birds flocked there to quench their thirst and to meet other birds in a festal environment, where not only bird species partook, but also many other species of the animal world. Boynao and Boipu saw the small fishes splashing around blissfully and also tiny living organisms through the clear blue water that reflected their images like the deep waters of the Loktak Lake. The birds were not perturbed to see the little boys. For their innocent looks bespoke human love and kindness. The birds descended on to the water, started to drink, splashed around, chirped and flew up and down as if to entertain their unexpected guests. Boynao and Boipu watched all this quietly. They were thrilled!

It was noon! And the sun was straight above them. Those days, time was determined by the position of the sun in relation to the surroundings of man. Even animals and birds follow this system today. Birds and animals flock to their nests and shelter just before sunset. Looking at the sun, Boynao said to Boipu, "Let's move further up now. We have to reach the ridge and return home today." "This place is like a paradise! Don't you think that we should spend sometime more here with the birds and enjoy its freshness," said Boipu. They both finally agreed to stay on a few more hours amid the beautiful wildlife and serenity offered by the place. Boynao found it easy to fall in line with the idea of his friend as the same emotions and feelings that overtook his friend had also overwhelmed him. This tiny lake for them was the nerve centre of the animal kingdom. Their intuition told them that the drama of all animals and birds dwelling this beautiful mountain would gradually unfold before their eyes. They heard tales of spirits of the Thangjing Hills and strongly believed that the influence of these spirits was responsible for the strange behaviours of animals and birds living there.

They looked for a vantage point from where they could observe the manifold wildlife activities. Finally, they selected a rock above the lake ever-watching the goings-on at this little paradise. The rock seemed to have been ensconced there since time immemorial and looked akin to rocks in the Biblical Land – same fabric as the temple pulled down by Samson after Delilah ditched him. After sometime, they heard the barking of a hog deer. They were amused by the sound and were a little nervous, at the same time. A few minutes later, it barked again, and it was right next to them. The deer didn't see them. The boys were hiding behind the rocks. A male deer was leading the herd. The tips of its antlers appeared in the bushes; the head popped out a few times. In no time, the herd arrived at the water point. One by one, the deer drank the water and quenched their thirst. The last of the herd to drink the water was another male deer with lovely antlers. Suddenly, two fowls descended upon the spot from above the big tree standing like a guardian to the living there, one perched on the right antler and another on the left. The birds whispered to the male deer leading the herd, and the animals moved out of the lake soon after. The birds continued to sit on the antlers as the male deer moved along with the herd towards the deep dark forest. The birds represent the spirits that rule the wild.

It was time to say goodbye to the place! The boys then started to walk up the mountain. They were tired and hungry. They had nothing to eat. After sometime, they came across banana trees, but the place was swarming with monkeys. The bananas were either half-eaten or torn to pieces. The boys dislodged the crafty and mischievous monkeys and picked up a few bananas and ate whatever was left for them by the monkeys. They regained their strength and began to resume the trek. It was nearing sunset when they reached the top. The ridge offered a spectacular view of the valley of Manipur, the Loktak and the breathtaking landscape. It was tempting to stay on at the top. There were huge stones in a triangular formation on the ridge. This looked like a piece of exquisite craftsmanship! They climbed atop the triangular rocks that resembled those unique ancient rock formations along the coast of Northern Ireland! They were filled with inquisitiveness. The view from atop the rocks answered them all!

The kids reluctantly climbed down the rocks slowly lest they fall down and get hurt. As they touched the ground, they saw a curl-shape giant python raising its head about four feet above the ground. This posture of the giant snake was very intimidating! The little boys prostrated before it and begged for mercy! The snake whispered to them not to be afraid. The snake told them that they were the first humans to ever visit its domain and worship it. "I am very pleased to see you little boys! I shall protect you and bless you", said the snake. The boys were still shaken. They then got up. With folded hands, Boipu said, "Ye! Great Creature, I bow before thee in adoration as my forefathers had always done unto thee!' The snake then took them to a tunnel below a rocky hillock a few metres down the ridge. There, the children saw glittering ornaments, precious stones and gems displayed in abundance. The snake asked them to take home a precious stone each and ornaments as much as they could carry. The kids were delighted! They picked up the stones and some glittering ornaments. The python said that the stones would bring them good luck! The snake took the kids back to the ridge and showed them the valley of Manipur and the

Loktak Lake and said that it was the proud master of the Land. The python blessed the kids and bade them goodbye.

Finally, it was time to descend the mountain. Boynao and Boipu thought they would complete the journey back home in a couple of hours, before the night got late and their parents got worried. This was not to happen! Darkness soon came upon them, and they lost their sense of direction. They held each other's hands so that they didn't get separated and land up in a more miserable situation. But, their journey was getting tougher by each passing minute! Suddenly, Boynao slipped on the slippy slope and took along his friend twenty feet down. They were shaken! They came across a small path and followed it until they came to a cave. The cave was surrounded by tall trees and there were shrubs, as well. They decided to spend the night there. There was, however, no other option!

Back in the village, their parents had anxious moments. The villagers started streaming into the homes of the little boys and soon swelled in number, each carrying a blazing torch. After sometime, the villagers searched the neighbourhood forest for the boys, but without success. The village folks kept vigil throughout the night. The scene resembled a restive night in modern-day Manipur! The village headman along with a few others left for Moirang at the peep of day for seeking military assistance from the contingent of the King's army that was stationed there.

In the cave, the little boys were scared! It was a moonlit night. However, the fear of darkness cast its shadow upon them! Suddenly, they heard noises, somewhat like the sounds produced by the flapping of leaves in the wind on a summer day. They looked around and saw a majestic deer standing right next to them under the trees. It was the Sangai! Moments later, they saw a herd of Sangai in the bush around the cave. The animals were friendly, and the boys felt homely. They also saw two fairies mounting a Sangai. The fairies were like miniature men and had small wings to fly. They were amused to see the little boys in a lonely forest where humans rarely ventured into. After awhile, the fairies dismounted the Sangai and reassured the kids. The boys reciprocated and talked to the fairies about their adventure. Boynao whispered to his friend, "I hope these two creatures won't do any harm to us tonight. I'm very scared!" Boipu replied, "You know, my grandparents used to narrate stories about fairies and most of them were about the good things fairies do. They said, 'Fairies are good spirits and never harm humans. They also protect animals, especially the weak ones so that the weak species do not become extinct from the surface of the earth'. Hence, I'm sure they are here to help us." After sometime, the fairies came back and brought them food. The boys were surprised to see the food brought in banana leaves like freshly cooked food served at their homes. They ate to their hearts' content as the Sangai looked on reassuringly.

The night was getting late! The little boys were tired. The fairies suggested that they should sleep and assured them that no harm would come to them. Barely when they started to sleep, they were awakened by the sound of a roaring tiger! The roar was so loud that it could be heard from a far distance. The fairies comforted the boys not to be afraid. They then alerted the Sangai herd. The deer quickly encircled the boys and were ready to take on the tiger. The fairies told the male Sangai to see to it that the boys were taken to another place in case the tiger got close to them. The fairies were believed to protect the small Sangai population living in the forest. This herd of Sangai left the Loktak many years ago for better pasture and some had even been killed by tiger until they met the fairies, who protected them by forewarning them of impending dangers. The tiger soon got close to them with its eyes burning brightly! The male Sangai with its long sharp antlers tried to ward off the tiger and was backed by other deer. The tiger would move backward and forward waiting for an opportunity to strike. This time, the tiger appeared to be interested in catching the two little boys. As the fight was on, the fairies mounted the boys on a Sangai and took them to a safer area away from the tiger. The male Sangai continued to engage the tiger in a fight. That was the only way to protect the little boys from the mighty predator!

The fairies, the little boys and the Sangai herd kept moving towards the Loktak leaving behind the brave Sangai who continued to fight the tiger all alone. It took them several hours to arrive at the foothills. They took great care to move at a safe distance from human habitation out of fear although the plains were mostly uninhabited. When they reached near the Loktak, the fairies told the boys the inevitability of parting ways as no humans would be able to live and survive in the lake. The boys rejoiced thinking of a reunion with their family! At the same time, they were sad thinking of separation. The fairies said to the boys, "You are safe here! This is human habited area. And we will go to the lake and dwell in it forever with the Sangai to be the pride and inspiration for man through the ages!" Moments later, the fairies mounted a Sangai. One by one, the Sangai herd raised their forelegs as they balanced their bodies on the phumdi and gracefully danced their way into the deep waters of the Loktak. The little boys watched tearfully as the herd of Sangai gradually danced away into the vast waters of civilization.

Later, the little boys were accorded a warm reception by the awestruck villagers, who listened to their tale of the Thangjing Hills. The contingent of the King's army searching for the little boys in the jungle spotted the brave wounded Sangai and was brought to their camp for nursing. The Sangai recovered miraculously! It was later taken over by the grateful villagers. The King who heard the adventure story of the kids visited the village to hear their tale and was exceedingly touched by the love, loyalty, bravery, sacrifices and selflessness that were manifested in man and animal relationship. As a gesture of honour and love, the villagers gifted the Sangai to the King! The kids also gifted the King a glittering stone! The priest, who accompanied the King, looked at the stone and said it was a lucky stone and would bring happiness, fortune and prosperity to the Kingdom. He also said that the King would become more and more powerful and his fame would soon spread far and wide. The King felt extremely proud! He rewarded the little boys with plenty of gold and silver. The King also gifted valuables to the villagers and recruited many of the village youths in the army. The village later became prosperous and famous. Boynao and Boipu later grew up to become powerful and trusted generals of the King's army. They raised their respective families and lived happily ever after.

SECTION–C

HAOFA, THE INDIGENOUS DOG OF MANIPUR (Tangkhul Dog/Awang Hui/Hao Hui)

'Haofa' is a rare breed of dog now found in Ukhrul District of Manipur. The term 'Haofa' is a compound word, the first word, 'Hao' generically meaning people from the Hills (Tangkhuls) and the 'fa' denoting 'dog' in local parlance. Literally translated, Haofa stands for 'Dog of the Tangkhuls'. It is widely believed that many years ago, this breed migrated along with the Tangkhuls to the Ukhrul District and the adjoining Tangkhul Somra tracts in Myanmar. It is said that a Haofa is owned by a royal family only. It can be transferred or sold to another royal family–royalty, however, would be measured as per prevailing conditions in Tangkhul society. It is also a status symbol in Tangkhul society.

The Haofa is considered a rare indigenous hound breed of Manipur due to its distinctive characteristics that make it special and different from other local dogs. There are two main breeds of Haofa, viz. Somra and Wangkhama. The Somra breed has a short thin black hair whereas the Wangkhama breed has black thin hair with a white stripe on the neck and chest. The most common colour of the dog is black, and black and white (white stripe around the neck, ventral area and tip of the limbs). The dog is medium to large in size and weighs between fifteen kilograms and twenty-five kilograms. It has typical dew claws at the ventral side of the limbs. It also has an amazing sniffing power and the spirit to adjust with any hunter or group of hunters. The Meiteis called the Haofa as 'Awanghui', meaning a tall and big dog.

The Haofa is also known by the skills it possesses. A bigger species of the Haofa, which performs the task of house guarding is known locally as 'Shimfa', meaning 'Homeguard'.

The Shimfa guards its master and his family members and properties. It sleeps near its master and could even recognize the footprints of its master and family members. The 'Safa' is smaller than 'Shimfa', but is an excellent hunter. The Safa has special qualities such as courage, agility, speed, strength and alterness that make it a superb hunter. Besides, the owner also imparts special training in the art of hunting. The Safa is a deadly dog; its small bite can even cause death to animals. These qualities make the Safa a hunter's choice over the Shimfa, that is comparatively slow and often takes pleasure in eating the animal it killed without its master's consent.

The Haofa is fondly reared by the Tangkhul Nagas as pet because of its gentleness, obedience and loyalty to its master. It also displays characteristics of bravery, independence and freedom. The Haofa is generally mild and gentle towards people and seldom barks. At the same time, it is ferocious and does not give in to other dogs easily.

Like any other dog, the Haofa prefers meat, but can also live on simple diet. The Haofa is given a royal treatment by its owner. The best food, including meat is given. Normally, unhealthy food like dead animal's meat is not given. The dog in the Tangkhul community is treated as a family member. Apart from hunting purpose, the dog is kept mainly as guard dog and for its ornamental value. The Haofa is very dear to the owner, and when it dies, it is given a royal burial. The death of Haofa marks a period of mourning for its owner and his family. The Haofa generally lives long and like other local breeds, its average life-span is over 10 years.

The proud owners of this dog usually cut the tip of the ears and amputate the tail of pups when they are thirty to forty-five days old. This is done to enhance its hearing ability, alertness and movement that are essential ingredients for a true Haofa. Besides, cutting is done to give the Haofa a stylish look, more strength and advantages while fighting with another dog. Dogs with long tails are generally vulnerable during fights.

The tail is cut with one stroke to give a clean-cut look.

There are tales about the hunting skills possessed by this breed–the ability to hunt in jungle for days with little food and the tenacity even to confront a tiger or lion in chance encounter while hunting. The following incidents, in which the Haofa had amply exhibited its courage, determination, tenacity and skills, are still talked about by village folks. In 1902, there was a hunter named Kr. Malungnei of Somdal village in Ukhrul District. He had a Haofa, a very brave hunting dog. One day, while he was hunting in the jungle, the villagers reported to him about the presence of a lion in that vicinity. At first, the hunter named above was reluctant to respond. After a while, he was, however, confronted with a difficult choice as he learnt that his dog was already after the lion's trail. Soon, the dog and the lion entered into a fierce fight. In order to save his dog from the jaws of the lion, the hunter charged the lion.The lion then turned towards him menacingly. Then and there, the dog bit the lion's hind-leg, provoking the lion to again make a pounce at the dog. At this juncture, the hunter speared the lion, grievously injuring it. This fight lasted for quite some time. At the end, the hunter was totally exhausted and could not further pursue the lion that limped away in the jungle. The following day, the lion was found dead near a small hut by a paddy field. Even today, the hunter's family is known in Somdal village as 'The Lion Family'. The tale of the Haofa and its master's loyalty and courage would continue to echo the Hills of Somdal for generations to come.

Another story centred around the hunting skill of a female Haofa owned by one RVS Shangrem of Somdal village. Even while the owner remained busy in day-to-day domestic works, the bitch would take her pups into the jungle for hunting. They would kill deer and then would return home to report to the master outcome of their hunting. The Haofa would jump up and pull the owner's garment to convey the message that it had killed an animal in the jungle. The owner would then follow the Haofa that would take him to the spot where the animal was killed. The owner would then collect the dead animal and bring it home. These stories were narrated by Mr Ngaishi Muivah, retd. Sr. Lecturer, DM College, Imphal.

The story of a female Haofa named Natu and her master N. Kapangso is fondly remembered in Nambasi, a remote village in Ukhrul District even today. Natu was a good and intelligent huntress and was able to easily discern an animal in a herd that its master set his eyes on. While on a hunting trip with her master in the forest, she would not get distracted by the animals like squirrel and rats and birds that she would come across, unless her master evinced some interest in them. Natu was the bread earner for the hunter's family and occupied a special place in their household. With the help of Natu, the master killed many animals such as deer, wild boar, bear, wildcat, monkey and birds. The master sold these animals and earned handsome amounts of money.

Natu gave birth to pups season after season and made her master and his family proud. And most of them later became very good hunters.

During a breeding season when Natu was expecting, her master decided to stay away from hunting activity all the while considering her condition. However, one day, he decided to undertake a hunting expedition and left for the forest quietly. Natu sensed it and followed her master stealthily. True to her profession, Natu soon trailed a wild boar and engaged the animal in a fierce tussle. The animal wounded the Haofa grievously. The master and other hunters soon got wind of the incident and rushed to the rescue of Natu. At home, she was cared for by her master's wife Lucy, who was in tears. In her last gesture of care, Lucy gave some water to Natu. Natu then faintly conveyed her gratitude to her master, moments before she slipped into another journey never to return. Kapang broke down and cried. He gave her a decent burial and a parting gun salute. This story was told by Mr MC John, Headmaster, Nambasi High School (retd).

The Haofa is useful to its master in many ways. In olden days, the owner would always take along the dog while travelling, as it has a strong power of observation and could warn its master of impending danger from man or animal. It barked when it sensed danger and thus helped its master in warding off the danger. In the past, the Haofa played a vital role in rites and rituals in Tangkhul society. In olden days, when an important person passed away, he was buried along with a live dog. Generally, the traditional graves of the Tangkhuls were deep and wide. There was a big hollow space inside the grave. The dog that was buried alive in the grave was provided with water and rice, enough to sustain him for a week. A bamboo pipe was also inserted into the grave for air to enter. All this was done in the belief that the dog would go to the land of the dead along with its master to secure the master from any kind of danger, as was the case when he was alive.

A girl marrying a boy from another village had to offer a dog to the local youths to secure permission to open the village gate so that she was allowed to leave the village with the bridegroom's party. In the past, in Tangkhul society, people used to feast on Haofa meat during send-off ceremonies of their daughters wherein blessings were invoked for them–an indication that the dog symbolises fertility.

Haofa's characteristics and temperament are vividly recorded in her memoirs entitled 'Naga Path' by Ursula Graham Bower. In the words of the writer, with the purchase of Haofa for a rupee, not a dog but a personality entered her household. He was, it was true, the hound of the old, true Naga breed; big, massive beast resembling chows. But nobody could have confused Khamba with a mere canine. His independence, his dignity, alone marked him as apart. By the time he was full-grown, he knew exactly where he came in the household; directly after the writer, but above the men, whom he treated always with an affectionate courtesy. He never fawned. Caresses he asked for when he wanted them, took, and departed. His life was lived in parallel with the writer's, together, but apart, as bachelor friends might share the same house. Yet he had, all the same, a sentimental and tender nature. He and the writer were deeply attached. Despite their one or two disagreements (such as over the question of the village goats), each went to the other for comfort in adversity, and his arrival did much to cheer her at that particular time. From this, it is observed that the Haofa is a loyal, friendly and extremely intelligent dog.

Today, the Haofa is little known to the outside world. Even among dog lovers in Manipur, this breed is not known much and not many people keep it as pet dog. Dr RK Satyendra Singh opined that the Haofa should be popularized and recognized as 'Indigenous Dog of Manipur' or else dog lovers of other states may start breeding it and later claim it to be their indigenous breed. *Dog lovers, awake!*

A white-striped Haofa

An Intimidating Visage

Loyal and Gentle

An Alert Haofa

A Duo of Black Haofa in Hunting Mode

The Dog Khamba with Luikai, Circa 1939, Ukhrul

BIBLIOGRAPHY

Keibul Lamjao National Park & Manipur brow-antlered deer (Cervus eldi eldi M'Clelland 1842) (A Panorama) by Dr Kh. Shamungou (Pub. by : Wild Life Wing, Forest Dept., Manipur).

Keibul Lamjao National Park – The Home of Sangai. Pub. by Forest Department, Manipur.

Brow-antlered Deer or Sangai (Cervus eldi M'Clelland, 1842) by SA Hussain, S. Singsit, N. Vaiphei, S. Angom and K. Kipgen.

Gee, E.P. 1955, The brow - antlered deer, Cervus Eldi M'Clelland Journal of Bombay, Nat. Hist. Soc. 52(4): 917-9.

Gee, E.P. 1960, Report on the status of brow - antlered deer of Manipur (India), Journal Bombay, Nat. Hist. Soc. 57(3):597-617.

Manipur Remote Sensing Application Centre

Gee, E.P. 1961, The brow - antlered deer of Manipur, Oryx 6(2): 103-115.

Management activities of Keibul Lamjao National Park by Wildlife Wing, Forest Department.

Wildlife Week Celebration 2007, Wildlife Wing, Forest Department, Manipur.

Wildlife Protected Areas in Manipur (2006-2007), Wildlife Wing, Forest Department, Manipur.

The Geography of Manipur by MT Laiba (book).

Haofa/Tangkhulfa/Awang Huijao by Ng. Luithui

Naga Path by Ursula Graham Bower Published by John Murray, 50 Albemar Lt. St. London (1st Edition-Oct. 1950, reprinted Feb. 1986).